Moving Forward In Life Despite Adversities

Stories and Poems

By

BONNIE LEE YOUNG

This book is a work of fiction. Places, events, and situations in this story are purely fictional. Any resemblance to actual persons, living or dead, is coincidental.

ISBN: 0-7596-4217-6 (softcover)
ISBN: 0-7596-4216-8 (electronic)

This book is printed on acid free paper.

1st Books - rev. 02/26/03

Long Row

INTRODUCTION

BY BONNIE LEE YOUNG

<u>*My Grandmother*</u>

With profound love and heartfelt devotion, I take pleasure in writing about the ones who moved forward in life despite adversities they faced. My grandma Isabella was one of them.

She was an American Indian born in the rural state of Georgia. Her best interest were in her children and grandchildren. With loving care she often gathered her grandchildren and sat them around her fireplace. She would sit at the head of them and filled with the desire to teach them the realities of life; how to deal with adversities as they come up while dealing with fellow humans.

One day she told her grandchildren how she became a slave. "My tribe did not surrender, so I was taken from my tribe and put with the slaves." Children, grandmother said, "slavery is not pleasant. It is a drudgery. You do as you are told."

She worked among those who hoed long cotton rows and sang religious songs. Although she worked among those who hoed long rows and sang religious songs, she held fast to her own religious teachings.

Eating Utensils

Grandma related to her grandchildren her eating utensils was not eating with forks or silver spoons. "I ate with my hands from the trough."

These are sayings of Grandma Isabella when we complained about what we didn't like. "Be thankful to God for what you do have and don't complain about what you don't have."

She never complained to her grandchildren about the adversities she faced in her life. Her words of wisdom were very encouraging.

Like one wise king said "On the lips of the understanding person wisdom is found." Proverbs 10:15.

You children should go to bed at night and thank God as you get up the next morning.

Grandma Isabella was a proud and dignified woman. That is why I call her a woman with a capital "W".

Married

Isabella married four times. Her first husband was Mr. Alexander. They brought forth two children, Merser and Will Alexander. Her next husband was Mr. Bland, and they brought forth Charles Bland. Her third marriage was to Mr. Hodges, and they brought forth Ludella and Villiola Hodges. Mr. Alexander, Mr. Bland, and Mr. Hodges all perished. Her fourth husband was Tobe Young. They brought forth five children: Sterling Young, Ross Young, Tip Young, Minnie Young, and Morrell Young. Through family research though, I was informed that the total number of children born to my grandmother was sixteen.

All of her offspring brought forth more children, giving her grandchildren. She took pride and time in teaching and telling her grand-children about their Indian heritage. She took no delight in telling her grandchildren the horrors of slavery. However, she taught us her history of slavery with love. She did not want us to have any hate or malice in our heart against people of other races. Her life was not centered on the material things only, but focused on spiritual goals. She was the first to inform the family about God's proper name. This was the foundation she laid for her offspring to look forward in life to worship the most high God. She believed in obeying the law of the land in a relative sense, and taught her grandchildren that it was essential to obey the law as well. She was a strong disciplinarian and stern in her teaching. Her yes meant *yes*, and no meant *no*! I remember one day we disobeyed my grandmother and she disciplined us with a rod.

I remember her saying these words: "When you have been taught right from wrong you don't go along with the crowd." And to this day I still apply those words in my life: 'don't follow the crowd.' Another teaching I appreciated was the traditional Indian way of making fires by rubbing two rocks together. She also taught us about time. She used the sun as an illustration, "when the sun rises, then you rise and shine." Another way she taught us about time was by your shadow. She said, when you can put your feet on your head that meant it was twelve o' clock. She also had a way to help you overcome complaining, "be thankful for what you already have, and don't look for what you don't have." When I was a young girl my traditional way of dressing was the style of a diaper. I was perplexed to hear about someone walking around with only a diaper and the top out, until I visited the Kolomoki Mounds. Then I said, "Grandma was right." I saw it all at the Mounds when I visit there.

Grandma Isabella was a woman who took pride in what she had established. She possessed many qualities such as modesty, humility, and love. She believed in one race, the Human race. She taught by examples, she believed in calling persons by their name only. Her electrifying speech was always clean and upbuilding, which is very different from the speech we hear today. By her example she gained respect from others. Isebella instilled a solid moral foundation in her children, which allowed them to move forward materially and spiritually possessing hundreds of acres of land. These things happened after each son got married and went their separate ways.

They were always helpful to each other despite the distance.

Tip, my father

The town they lived in was Georgetown, Georgia, and Fort Gains, Georgia, which was considered a farm territory. Isabella's son, Tip Young, married Jossie Smith in 1924. They got married in the house above on the front porch. After their wedding, Tip had taken his bride to his mother's home. My mother said Isabella welcomed her to her home. She said it was the first time she was accepted with favor and treated with loyalty. Tip and Jossie lived with Mother Isabella for a little while and then moved to a wealthy plantation. My father Tip, farmed for many years and he did very well. He planted peanuts, sweet potatoes, corn, cotton and more. He was the plantation owner's right hand man. He also helped others to come and work on the plantation including his sister, her husband and their children. Tip's wife, Jossie's brother and family, were also workers on this plantation. Tip and the plantation owner were more than just sharecroppers. They were friends. They worked and shared alike. The plantation owner was very nice to the workers that farmed on his land. He was loving, caring and had empathy for them. He never worked them too hard.

While living on the plantation Tip and Jossie brought forth nine children: Rubie, Cleo, Wendy, David, Isabella, Brownie, Tip Jr., Vera, and Willie. At this time Isabella was well along in age. She came to live with us. She spent her time between her son Tip and her daughter Minnie. Her last stay was at her daughter Minnie's home where she had taken sick. Every morning when I was on my way to school, I would stop by to see how Grandma Isabella was doing. I stood by her bedside and looked at her as she was looking up at the ceiling. I would say to her "Grandma when are you coming home?" She would never answer me. I did not realize how sick my grandmother was. I asked my mother when grandmother was coming back to live with us and mother's response was that she was not, because she was too sick. Then I asked my mother, "can't she be sick and live with us?" My mother just smiled at me because she knew how much I loved my grandmother.

Soon after, she died at 99 years of age. All of the family members attended the funeral of my grandmother, including the children. This was the first time that I experienced a funeral because my mother did not permit the younger children to these affairs, however, because of the closeness between my grandmother and I, we were allowed to attend. I cried throughout the service and my mother sat across from me looking and smiling with me. She was amazed that at my young age that I was able to discern the beauty and insight my grandmother displayed in life. I could not understand why grandmother had to die and leave us. After the funeral everyone returned home but grandmother's memories was still with us. The impression my grandmother left was great, because my mother patterned her lifestyle after her. Her teachings was very effective, because it stayed with us throughout our generations.

Persecution

I was born October 2, 1939 to Jossie and Tip Young. My sister Rubbie told me that I was persecuted the very first day I was born. I asked her how? She said the midwife took you away from the bed from my mother and put you in another bed away from our mother, it was very cold that day. The window was open and cold air was blowing in. Our mother was very sick and was unable to do anything. By the time our father got home from work I was very sick with a high fever, runny nose and tears running from my eyes. The midwife put a thin gown on me instead of a winter gown. Our daddy wanted to know what was wrong with me. The midwife smooth talked our daddy and told him that our mother did not cooperate with the procedure of the birth. Then I asked my sister what did my mother say? She said our mother was very sick and weak. Rubbie said, "You know what it is like when someone is very weak, they cannot defend themselves or speak with any power. The most they can do is signal". Then I asked my sister "How was I helped?"

Rubbie said that they had taken me to a doctor in Georgetown. His name was Doctor Gary. He treated me and said I was a healthy baby, but that I would be affected for the rest of my life because I did not get the proper medical care at birth. I asked Rubbie what happened after the doctor's visit. She said a few weeks later, you were o.k. The people in the neighborhood learned that I was a brown skinned chestnut colored baby. They all came to visit my mother and her new baby. All the visitors commented on what a pretty brown baby I was. Our mother said, "Since she was born a brown baby, let us name her Brownie!" They all agreed and clapped with exultation.

Daddy's profit

My father kept the same midwife

When I became two years old my mother gave birth to another baby boy. He lived only a few minutes and died. The reason for his death is that the midwife did not take the umbilical cord from around his neck in time. My father did not listen to our mother when she said the midwife was being mean to her and that she tied the bellyband on too tight around her belly.

Mother said when the midwife would leave, she would take off the bellyband herself. When the midwife would come in she would put the bellyband back on my mother's belly very tight. Mother said over and over she would tell my daddy about these occurrences and he would say, "Listen to the midwife, she knows what she is doing". In those days the younger people would listen to the older ones. When the baby died he fired this midwife. He was so hurt because Tip Jr. looked just like him. Depending on the circumstances it is good to listen to advice, but in this case it was not advantageous. When the baby was being taken away, I cried and said, "Let me hold the baby," but they just took him away and I did not get to hold him. I dreamed about him many nights but he would get away from me before I could reach him.

Our House

We lived a half a mile from the road in a four-room house. The house had a tin roof. When it rained we would enjoy the raindrops. We were surrounded with beautiful green trees, flowers, and the sight and sounds of the birds. We had chickens and roosters that I loved to hear crow. We had no running water in the house but we lived beautifully. We retrieved our water from the spring, and we loved carrying the buckets of water on our heads. We had two fireplaces to keep us warm in the wintertime. We all ate together including our mother and father. Mother would cook fresh food every day. She cooked on a wooden stove. We never went hungry.

Our father was a good provider and a good shepherd. He was a farmer, a fisherman, and my mother worked side by side with him. I love my father for being the man that he was. He showed love to all of his children, and never showed any partiality among us. What took me by surprise was that one Sunday we were all at a meeting, and my father was talking to two ladies. So I approached my father and said, "excuse me, I would like to have some money to buy some ice cream daddy." And, when I called him daddy, the two ladies that were talking to him looked down on me, and looked up at my daddy and said, "who is this dark-skinned girl calling you daddy?" He told them that I was his daughter, and the two ladies said, "you know this dark-skinned girl is not your daughter." My father gave me affection and rubbed his hand over my head, saying, "she is my daughter, she's dark like her mother." The two ladies looked at each other and made facial expressions. That was the first time I ever heard idiotic talk from people about color. I felt so good inside knowing that my father did not deny me because of my skin color.

Not only did my father show affection toward me, but mister Lokey, his plantation owner, did also. One day while I was playing hopskip, the plantation owner asked my father if I could be his daughter's permanent playmate. My father said, "I will permit my daughter to play with your daughter as long as you like, but not permanently." They both laughed it off. They had a good relationship. Mr. Lokey could have asked for any one of my sisters to be his daughter's playmate, but he asked for me. I became her playmate, mostly in her home. Her mother, Mrs. Lokey dressed me as well as she did her own daughter. They treated me like I was one of theirs. They never spoke the kind of idiotic talk that I had heard once before, but they treated me with love.

I thought that one of their sons did not like me. One day Mrs. Lokey asked one of the boys to fix me and Mary lunch. He poured his sister's glass full first, then he poured mine half way, and looked at me and smiled, and then he filled my glass up full, making sure that my glass was equal to hers. I thought that was so loving. Her oldest son Richard would carry me to and from her house. Mrs. Lokey would say to him, "be careful." "Make sure no snake bites her." By the love they showed to me, I did not have an inferiority complex about my color despite what others had said.

Education

My father only went to the third grade but his education did not stop there. He was self-taught in the subject of law. He was very good at law and poetry. My mother left school at a very young age because the teacher elevated his voice at her and she was afraid to go back. She received further knowledge from those who taught her the Bible. My father made certain that his children received an education, and we did. I had a learning disability, but my mother would say, "although you have a learning disability, don't be down or sad about it, because I am going to keep you in school as long as I live. You still have dignity, because God made all of us with intelligence. Don't feel left out because you have this problem. Just stick with it and go forward." I do just that down to this day. I currently take classes at New York University where I write stories and poetry. Doing this has been very helpful and beneficial to me.

Family

As we grew in number, my father continued to farm with Mr. Lokey. The land was very productive. Fruit trees of all sorts were there. But our next tragedy while there on the farm was our beautiful sister, Wendy, was burned to death. She was visiting her friend, and they were all playing with a record player, and her back was turned to the fireplace. She was wearing one of those flair skirts that she loved. A spark from the fireplace caught her dress and set it afire. She got excited when that happened, and started running, but no one could catch her. The wind was blowing very hard that day. While she was yelling, the wind blew the flame down her throat. They sent for doctor Gary, and he came to treat her. He said there was no help for her because she had swallowed the flames. That is what killed her. She was just nine years old.

You wouldn't believe that I was just two, but I remember all of this. The next morning we all stood around her bed, but she had expired. My sister had a different name given to her when she was born, one that I did not like. I did not like my sister given name at birth, so I renamed her Wendy. I renamed her Wendy, because the day of her death it was very windy. She also carried me with her everywhere she went. I was her doll.

As time went on, my father was able to cope with my sister's death. He continued to dwell with Mr. Lokey, who encouraged him to stay on. An agreement was made between the two that my father stay on despite the tragedy that happen. As time went on my father said he wanted to move forward and prepare for his sons, he did just so. He bought his own plantation, and moved forward. But before we moved from that plantation my mother became very ill with cancer. When we moved to our new house, she only saw two of the rooms in the house, she was too weak to go any further, we had to put her back in bed. My father wanted to put her in the hospital, but she did not want to go there. She wanted to stay home and look after her children. I couldn't understand why my mother did not want to go to the hospital at that time. However, when I grew older and became a mother myself, I understood.

Later, before her death though, she agreed to go to a hospital in Columbus, Georgia. I had stayed home from school that day and went with my father to the hospital to see my mom. As my father was waiting to hear the report from the doctors, I was standing by my mother's side, even though she was very weak, she pointed out to me, "never go with a married man." The lady in the bed next to her was the talk of the hospital. While she was well and on her feet, she would run through other women's husbands. But, like the Bible says, "You reap what you sow." Now, she was laying on her back in a hospital bed, and her beauty could not make her well. I kept this in front of me throughout my life. Finally, the doctor called in with a report to the nurse. The report stated that there was nothing more they could do for my mother, the cancer had progressed too far. So, we took her home from the hospital that very same day. My mother died from the cancer a few weeks later, at home, I was fifteen.

My oldest brother Cleo, his wife Ozzie, and their two sons, Cleo Jr. and David came with us when we moved from Georgetown, Georgia to Fort Gaines. Cleo came along for the purpose of helping my father run the farm. Ozzie was very good to us. She was both our sister-in-law, and our mother. My oldest sister Rubbie was already married and had left the house. Isabella, Vera, Willie, David, and myself remained in the house. Six months after my mother's death, my father got married to Ozzies' aunt Lillie. Then, trouble started in the house. Ozzie and her aunt Lillie didn't get along, so my brother decided that to avoid any further trouble, he would leave. He left the house for about six months and farmed elsewhere. He later returned, and is still present there today.

"Cleo tells his experience about farming. "Farming today" Cleo said, "is much easier then farming were in the 40s. When I was farming with my father we did not have the modern day machinery like they have today." "We plowed with a mule to break the soil of the ground to get ready for planting the seed in the ground." "We got up early in the morning and shine, shine to the evening come." Although the work were hard, and we faced adversities. We continued on until we reached our goal. Now the land is paid for. I got the deed and the land is mine. On the other hand I kept in mind the advice my father gave me. "Son pay your taxes by doing so you wont have no trouble with the government." I truly can say that to obey is better then a sacrifice. Now we are enjoying life with a smile. Thanks to God and thank to my father for making life better for us."

Woe

Next, Mrs. Lil brought trouble throughout the whole household. She encouraged my father to put us on the farm and make us work, to pick those velvet beans that have the sticky peel on them. She told my father that he would save money by making us work the farm instead of hiring workers. When my father would go and make deals with different companies to sell, he wouldn't be home when we came back from the field. Her way of cooking was very different from my mother's way of cooking. One day she cooked, and put salt in the sweet potatoes, and told us to eat it. My sister Isabella (whom we called Daisy for short), was facetious. She went in the kitchen, and took over. She said, "Get out of this kitchen. I'm going to feed my sisters the way my mother cooked for us." And that's what my sister did, she fed us. When my father got home from taking care of business, Lillie made him whip us for disobeying her. As time went on, her domineering ways got worse. Then, all of us started to leave home. David left first to get a job to help out my father with the farm. Next, Daisy left, then I left after her, and Vera after me. Willie was the last to leave. He stayed and helped my father quite a bit with the farm. Isabella went to Columbus Ohio.

I came to New York, but New York did not meet my expectations. I didn't want to return home because of my domineering stepmother. I worked in factories, I was a nanny, I worked in department stores like Tailored Woman on Fifth Avenue, and other jobs. Six months after I arrived in New York, I was married to Willie Lee. He went into the Marines shortly after we were married. I continued to stay with my aunt, and I worked. He went overseas for about eighteen months, then I lived on base with him for a while in Jacksonville, North Carolina. There we conceived a son. Then I moved from Manhattan to the Brooklyn Navy Yard, where my husband was stationed. Then I told him that I wanted to go to school to be a barber.

He agreed. I furthered my education at Tyler Barber college in New York City. I practiced barbering for twenty-seven years. I managed a shop for four years. The same shop that I managed for four years, I owned for eight years. This came about when the owners of the shop failed to pay their taxes. I payed the taxes, and the shop came to be mine. I love barbering. The only thing I didn't like about barbering was that when I met beautiful people, they would leave and go to another town. I would not see them anymore.

to Miss Young
the best
Sonny Rollins

When I was living in Georgia, I was working on my father's farm and heard an airplane flying in the sky. I wondered what it was like, flying in the sky. From that experience, I had a strong desire to fly. When I turned eighteen, I got a job and saved my money. A few years passed and I was on Australia's Airline, July 1, 1965 from New York to Vienna, from Vienna to Zurich, from Zurich to Basel from Basel to Frankfurt from Frankfurt to Berlin, Amsterdam, Brussels, London, from London to New York, JFK. I said, to myself, could this Georgian country girl be flying to Europe for three weeks? My mind reflected on what my mother said, "Brown you can be successful in life as long as you are honest, honest to yourself and to others. Sometimes it takes years. Think and be wise and do not let your left hand know what your right is doing and you will be successful in life." So I did just so, and I was successful in flying. Many times on different Airlines, On America, Delta, Eastern, TWA airlines, Europe and QANTAS, Australia's airline.

Barbering helped me to travel to see quite a bit of the world. I traveled throughout Europe, to Mexico City, Acapulco, Canada, the Caribbean, San Juan Puerto Rico, The Virgin Islands, Bermuda, and Barbados. Barbering helped me to meet famous people. One that I like was Sonny Rollins, the saxophone player. I was his private barber for about five years. I also met Savannah Churchill's son, as well as others. When the building was sold the new owner wanted his storefront, so I had to go elsewhere to work. I worked in Manhattan for a well-known hair stylist, where I continued there until I had developed a vein occlusion in my eye. I loved barbering, but I could no longer continue to practice barbering. But during my time as a barber I did not invest any money, I enjoyed life by flying and seeing the different countries that I longed to see when I was young. Because of the vein occlusion I had to collect my retirement benefits and social security. I am happy at the present time.

Isabelle

Isabelle

Let me tell you more about my sister Isabelle. As I stated earlier she was a very facetious person, she was beautiful, had natural curly hair, brilliant and did not hold back on her words. Whatever fit your feet you would have to wear it. Before we learned about death from anyone else, she was the first to tell us. She spoke very blunt and did not have any mercy on how it would affect us.   You see, what happened, my mother's cousin's son died, and his brother came to tell our mother about his death. At this time our mother was not home, so he bestowed the bad news upon us and departed. Now, Isabella told Vera and myself that we were going to die. So Vera and I started crying all throughout the evening. She told us that we were going to deteriorate. I knew that animals died but not people. Now, my mother had arrived home and we told her that Isabella told us that we were going to die and asked her if this was true, but she just smiled at Vera and I, and did not reply. Being that mother gave us no reply I suspected that she felt it was not time for us to know. As I became an adult I found out why we die and so did Vera. Her facetiousness did not stop there but she carried it on when she left Georgia and resided in Columbus, Ohio.

Her daughter related to me in these words.

I was born on September 18, 1949 to Isabella Young in Columbus, Ohio to live with her great aunt Miss Carrie Williams and her husband Frank Williams.

When I was two years of age, my aunt Carrie Williams and her husband. My mom (Carrie) told me that when I was an infant that my birth mother did not want me and that she had promised me to a nurse at the doctors office and to a neighbors family. My great, great aunt Carrie told me that she wanted to keep me in the family so she and her husband decided to adopt me.

Mom said when I was an infant, I used to cry for my birth mother but she wanted nothing to do with me. I remember very little about my first two years. Things that I can recall are things that my mom shared with me. You see, at that time, I did not know my birth mother was Isabelle. My first memories started at the age of three or four. I remember going to an East Market St. Vernon Ave, in Columbus, Ohio with my mother to visit her brothers fruit and vegetable stand every week. They would let me give change to the customers. I remember that Isabelle worked at a meat market called Herb's Ballou's, and I would visit every one in the market when I was there. I recall moving to our new home in East Gate and started school at East Gate Elementary School, at that time East Gate was where the middle and upper middle class blacks lived.

My first memories of elementary school were when I was in the third grade. I had a beautiful teacher by the name of Mrs.Cox. I knew then that I wanted to be like her. In my fourth grade year I went to the room of what I thought was the meanest teacher alive, Ms. Ruth Clement. She was very tall and had beautiful long nails. If you got into trouble with her, your butt was grass, as they say. And as luck would have it, since I loved to talk, I got into a little trouble. Ms. Clement saw something in me that I did not see in myself, she encouraged me to be sensitive. And boy did I try. When I was growing up, it was difficult because my adopted mother was up in age of sixty years when I was ten. I had no sisters or brothers to talk with or confide in so I became some-what closed. I remember mom used to mention Bonnie and she always would call and talk to me, but she never told me who she was until later in life.

The other parents in our neighborhood always socialized with each other and the other children of these families all belong to "Jack and Jill," and pretty much stuck together. While my school friends were having fun spending the night at each other houses going skating and doing kids things, I was at home watching TV with mom wondering why. I could never understand. I always wanted to fit in but it seemed I never could, Some girls did not like me because they said 'She thinks she is cute because her mom buys her nice clothes and she has long pretty hair' others did not like me because they called me names like half breed. Although in school I would try out for different things. Clubs, cheerleading, choir, track, you name it. During my elementary years I rarely remembered Isabell's presence. Except when she chased me around the house yelling at me to do some housework. When I turned twelve, that was the day I found out who Isabell really was. On that day she announced her engagement to Eugene Holmen and he wanted me to know the truth, so they finally told me. I was angry because all those years of confusion, lacked a motherly conversation, curiosity, and I could have used some good advice. Don't get me wrong, my adopted mother gave me all that she could, but for a child in my era, I needed much more.

Around the sixth grade, I developed the biggest crush on the neighborhood's cutest guy, Larry Davis. When I finally reached junior high school we both had a crush on each other. I tried out for cheerleading, then track and choir, made it and quickly became accepted into the in crowd! In junior high school my friendship started to grow and my relationship with my childhood sweetheart grew stronger, but rocky. He moved!! My relationship with Isabell began to grow worse. It was as if she hated me. She treated me terribly during those days. The more I tried to get to know her, the worse she treated me. During those years Isabelle became more and more hostile toward me and she began to drink more and more. By the time I reached the ninth grade she would talk. She would talk of her family in Georgia, her land in Georgia, but she was quick to tell me, I would never see them or the land. I always wondered who was my family, who was my father, my grandfather, my grandmother, and cousin. Did I have any sisters or brothers? When I reached high school, things got progressively worse, by now my adopted mother was seventy years old. I could only associate with my Ohio cousin. I was not allowed to go to house parties or slumber parties. When all my schoolmates were skating at Rollerland (where the black kids went) I was skating at Smith's Roller Rink to organ music where the whites went. I HATTTTTEEEEDDDDD ITTTT! Mom just would not and could not understand today's teenagers. I was constantly seeking acceptance from everyone and everything. Isabella began to drink more and more and became more and more verbally abusive. She always threatened to hurt me physically, and by now, I hated her as well, or so I thought. I really wanted her to love me.

Times were tough in high school, some of the girls who lived in another area just did not like any one from East Gate. I got teased unmercifully, harassed, laughed and lied on. The sad part was that I tried to like everyone, but only to be ridiculed. Some days I wanted to fight the world, but could not do anything about it because in those days if you got into a fight, you were kicked off the drill team, cheerleading squad or track team, etc. I had many disappointments during those days. My life long childhood sweetheart was the heartthrob of many and I was but a fleeting thought, "So I thought". We broke up and got back together constantly and Isabell's life was quickly getting out of control with her drinking and fighting.

By the twelfth grade I decided to go for a new guy, since I wanted to be popular, I dated the infamous popular guy. They called him "Stinkey. "Half way through my senior year I was tired and fed-up with everything and everybody, so I started making friends from other communities. I made a bad choice of friends and was raped in November of my senior year. I never told my adopted mother, but I told my boy friend. He consoled me and started to protect me and showed me the love I thought I longed for. So I decided to let someone love me. You probably guessed that I became pregnant at age seventeen. Isabell blew a fuse and attempted to fight me. She would accuse me of taking her things and her money. By now, I had such a dislike for her it did not matter and remember throwing her over a dresser and told her to leave me alone. From that point on I would never

come to my adopted mother's house if she were there.
I got married at seventeen and divorced at eighteen. I
had a girl.

I finished high school and went on to college part-time. It took me forever, but I did finally finish.
Between the age eighteen and twenty-one I ran wild. I
wanted to do all the things I never could and see
something of the world. By my twenty-first birthday I
was tired of the popular guys so I started to date a
regular Joe. I got married and had two more children,
but the marriage was very abusive. Many days I had
black eyes and bruises. After nine years I left. My
mom told me the children could stay with her, but I
could not because I felt I should stay married for the
sake of the children. I left anyway with nothing. I
lived in my car for a couple of months and stayed at

friend's houses. When I got my first apartment, I had nothing but a mattress on the floor and a plastic fork and knife.

I had a few successes but I always seemed to slide backwards. I had no support from the children's fathers and I hated my jobs. In 1980 my birth mother became sick and died. It was not until then, the day before her death, that she told me that she loved me for the first time. I think that was a wonderful moment for me to have my mother love me and that was my first meeting of my true family. I was so happy to finally feel that I belonged somewhere. I have the greatest aunts and uncles. My only regret is not being able to grow up with them. My aunt Bonnie never lost track of me, she always kept in touch, and to this day, I am glad she did.

Although the years were turbulent, and my hate for my mother has slowly turned to love, I regret we never had a chance to share that love for each other. But the good part is when I looked at my Aunt Bonnie and Aunt Vera, I see my mother and I feel her love. There is still a piece of the puzzle that I am searching for, but that's still secret.

Today I have a wonderful family. My husband Kirk Wooding has been the love of my life and Stella should have called me I could have told her about the groovy things along time ago. I have five wonderful children. Gina, Kyra, Michael, Kacie, and Kirk, whom I love dearly and unconditionally. Throughout all my problems I have been blessed with a lovely home in Georgia. My beautiful house, my beautiful children and I thank God that I'm looking forward to serve him now.

Mr. And Mrs. Woody Young   Our home in Atlanta, Ga.

House

Then we moved away from the Lokey plantation to historical Fort Gaines, Georgia. Our house was not as nice as the house we lived in on the Lokey plantation. Not that we did not appreciate what our father did for us, we were very grateful what he did. He did just what a loving father would do. The problem was we were disappointed with the house when we looked up at the ceiling and see the stars at night.

We said many times only if our mother were living things would be better because she always went for the best of everything, the best or nothing. She worked very hard and saw that everything went well with our daddy.

They loved each other very much. And they showed it. Not only to themselves, but to others and here work was around the clock. If she wasn't working with dad, she was busy making our clothes and teaching us about God.

Fort Gaines Fort and Bonnie looking out

Bonnie, Kirk, Kacie

Kacie   **Bonnie**

Gina

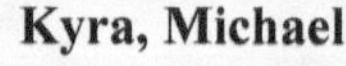

Kyra, Michael

Kacie

Kirk Jr.

My Dear One Arrives

My dear one has arrived from a distant land.

He embraces me and tells me:

"You are beautiful my dear one. You are so beautiful.

You are sweeter than cherry wine and I know you are

mine.

Like the dew falls from heaven and saturates and

refreshes

the field

so do your eyes saturate and refresh my mind.

King Solomon said the most magnificent words of all,

but, honeycomb, you are my all.

Dust rises, rises and rises and dusts the sky,

but dust will not rise over my eyes for you.

Like the sun rises and shines over the earth,

so does my love shine over you.

Hurricane rises up and overfloods oceans and rivers,

but hurricanes will not overflood my love for you.

Because my love for you is deeper than any ocean and

wider

than any sea. And no one can take away my love from

you.

"Sweet cherry, honey plum, will you marry me?"

"Yes, my dear one. My heart is overflowing for you.

I'll be

yours forever.

"Yes, my dear one, my heart heard your voice from a

distant land."

HA, HA, HA, look before you leap.

12/30/99 Lesson from the Rabbit

One day Bunny Rabbit was feeling very, very good. So he decided he would take a walk to Mr. Brown's farm. When he reached Mr. Brown's farm he stared in amazement at the beautiful farm. So much so, he danced and he danced until he was off balance and fell in Mr. Brown's well. After he fell in Mr. Brown's well, Bunny Rabbit could not get himself out of the well. Then suddenly Bunny Rabbit heard Bro Fox's voice. So he called up to Bro Fox to get him out of the well. Bro Fox said, "How?" Bunny Rabbit said get in the bucket and come down and get me out. Bro Fox was so hungry and desperate to eat Bunny Rabbit, he did not think what Bunny Rabbit was up to. So he jumped in the bucket and went down to get Bunny Rabbit to eat him. But he was disappointed so he called for Bunny Rabbit to bring him back up. Bunny Rabbit said this is the way the world is. Everyone is going their own way. Wake up and stay awake, that is what I did.

8/22/2000

BRIANNA

Brianna tells me.   Her grandmother tells her these words…

Brianna doesn't like me much and this is how I

know; I hold outstretched arms to her and she just

tells me "no." So patiently I wait until she needs a

favor

from me.

And then I go and fetch for her as fast as I can run or

when her mama says it's time for her to take a nap I

sometimes plead—I really do, want to hold her on my

lap. And there's even been a time or two when

discipline was due that my entreaties saved the day.

As her affection I'd pursue. Now you may think that

it's not wise to gain her love this way,

but if it works, I'll tell you this, I'll do it anyway. All

dressed up and ready to go she stood waiting at the

door. A vision of loveliness this pretty little girl of four.

Her golden curls lay softly

around her dainty face then tumbled gently down her

back with amazing grace. A full white petticoat

beneath a pink pinafore with yards of lace adorn the

pretty little girl of four with legs all swathed in soft

pink lace.

And shiny black shoes upon her feet. My eyes delight

in all they see of this little girl so very sweet. But, as

my eyes caress this lovely sight, something there is

not quite right. Her right shoe is on the left foot and

the left is on the right.

12/7/99

My Dark and Rocky Road

Early one morning about the break of dawn, my room was very, very quiet and not a sound was heard and suddenly I heard a voice saying wake up and rise and walk your dark and rocky road. You paid your rent but your rent will not save your life. So get up and walk your dark and rocky road. My heart was jumping like I was hit by a millstone. I could not hold my breath. I sat down on the side of the bed to take a deep breath then the voice of a woman said no. You do not have not one minute. You leave hear with just what you have on. Your dark and rocky road is all prepared for you. So get up and walk your dark and rocky road.

I got up and walked out of the door and I was directed straight to a crossroad. When I reached the crossroad I could not see before my eyes because it was jet black outside and suddenly a bright light flashed by like lightning. The light was so bright I could not see how to walk my dark and rocky road. Before I started to walk my dark and rocky road. I was lifted up and put on the dark and rocky road and then I heard a voice saying "Do not look back and do not look to the left or right. "Keep walking with your head up and look straight ahead and walk your dark and rocky road.

So I walk and walk my dark and rocky road. Yes I walk my dark and rocky road with nothing to hold on to and no one to hold my hands. At least that's what I thought. But yet I walk with admiration. Yes. I walk my dark and rocky road. When I came to the end of my dark and rocky road, I look across the road and I saw a crowd of women and one of the ladies said, "that looks like Bonnie." And another lady looked around and said "Let her stay on the dark and rocky road. She does not belong with us." Before I knew it a hand lifted me up and put me on the bright road. Than I heard voices singing like a chorus of birds.

The song they were singing was "you can see with your eyes people are dwelling together. Sorrow has passed, peace at last. No more tears and pain." And now you can sing along with the others. "Thanks to our God. Our Maker. Life without end at last." From this we all can see that we all have something to work on. We can see from the above words it's not what man sees, but what God sees. Yes. Yes I walk. I walk my dark and rocky road.

Bonnie Lee Young

A dark and rocky road.

7/27/2000

FLAMES

My dear one,

The night is well on the way, and the chickens are at roost and the foxes are in their den. Let us take a walk through the forest and listen to the whistling pine trees and express our love to each other. My dear one you are so beautiful and you are sweeter than cherry wine and you are the lady of my heart.

I spent many restless nights longing to rest my head between your beautiful breasts at night. Will you marry me?   Yes

My dear one, the way you express your love to me. It motivated me to tell you my love for you is so intensifying, so much so it is like flames of fire blazing over the twin tower and cannot be put out.

My dear, my love for you is so great it is a phenomenon and only Jehovah can make this phenomenon possible. The same as He did for Jacob and Rachel. If He sees fit to do so. My dear one, my love for you is the greatest thing ever to happen to me.

My dear one, my love for you is like blazings and blazings of fire like the flame of Jah, and cannot be put out. The wise king said many waters themselves are not able to extinguish love, nor can rivers themselves wash it away if a man would give all the valuable things of his hourse for love, person would positively despise them. The Song of Solomon 8:7.

Bonnie Lee Young

8/3/98

LIKE THE SUN RISES AND

SHINES, I SHINE

YOU EXAMINED MY EYES

AND YOU PRONOUNCED

ME BLIND BUT DID I

FROWN? NO, I SHINE.

YOU MADE ME YOUR SLAVE.   NOW YOU

ARE WAITING YOUR GRAVE, DID I DIG

YOUR GRAVE? NO, I SHINE.

YOU DID NOT PRONOUNCE MY SONG,

STILL YOU DID ME NO HARM, LIKE THE

SUN RISES AND SHINES, I SHINE.

YOU BROKE MY CROWN AND YOU TRIED TO BLOW ME DOWN, BUT DID I DROWN? NO, I SHINE.

YOU KNOCK ME DOWN AND YOU DID NOT FROWN, STILL I SHINE.

YOU PRONOUNCED ME BLIND, BUT YOU DID NOT PRONOUNCE MY TIME, BECAUSE WITH GOD THERE IS NO LIMIT ON TIME. SO I SHINE, SHINE, SHINE, TO THE END OF SATAN'S TIME.

I SHINE, SHINE, SHINE, TILL HE IS BINDED AND GOD HAS KNOCKED HIM DOWN.

LIKE THE SUN RISES AND SHINES, I SHINE, SHINE, SHINE.

*AND AT THE END OF SATAN'S TIME, GOD WILL GIVE ME MY CROWN, AND **I SHINE, SHINE, SHINE.***

8/3/98

THE WATER LILY POOL

THE WATER LILY POOL IS SO BEAUTIFUL. WOULD YOU LIKE TO LIVE THERE? AND WOULD YOU LIKE TO GO AND LOOK AT THE LILIES? LILIES MAKE YOU DREAM ABOUT THE ONE YOU LOVE. REMEMBER WHAT ONE WISE MAN WROTE ABOUT THE LILIES OF THE FIELD. HE QUOTED WHAT A SHEPHERD BOY SAID TO HIS BRIDE. THE SHEPHERD BOY SAID TO HIS BEAUTIFUL BRIDE: "YOU ARE BEAUTIFUL. LIKE THE LILIES AMONG

Bonnie Lee Young

THE THORN WEED, SO IS MY DEAR ONE

AMONG THE DAUGHTERS OF MEN."

Compare

One wise man said

The way a tree falls is the way it lies.

The way a man lives, is the way he dies.

The people in the world are like that lying

tree.

They do not have anyone to love them, or

care for them.

People need love, justice, peace, empathy.

People need someone who care about

People's needs in order

To help them in a loving way.

So they can be nourished back to life.

11/23/98

Bonnie Lee Young

2/1/00

FAVOR

WHEN WE NEED A FAVOR WHO DO WE ASK?

Someone we know, a friend, or someone we have confidence in.

Of course, someone we have confidence in.

Someone who can see and feel our needs.

But why do we forget the one who fulfilled and satisfies our needs.

Have you not heard, that the bridge that carried you across will carry you across again if it is still standing.

So why not be grateful to someone who did you a favor and show appreciation, because it is rewarding.

Proverbs 25:11 says, "As apples of gold in silver carvings, is a word spoken at the right time for it."

Do Not Fold the Pages of Love From Your Fellowman's

When you find a dear loved one, you have
found a jewel.

Love and cherish your dear loved one.

But when you have found a dear loved one

Please do not fold the pages of love from your

fellowman's

Because when you fold one page of love from

your fellowman's,

You have folded all the pages of love from

yourself.

Love one another.   No one has love greater

than this

that someone should surrender his soul

On behalf of his friend."

John 15:12-13

Bonnie Lee Young

A WORD OF WISDOM TO YOUNG PEOPLE

I THINK YOUNG PEOPLE ARE BEAUTIFUL.

BUT THEY NEED SOMEONE TO LOVE AND CARE FOR THEM.

SOME PARENTS DO A GOOD JOB IN RAISING UP THEIR CHILDREN AND THEY SET A GOOD EXAMPLE FOR THEM. SO WHAT IS THE CHILDREN'S PROBLEM?

THE CHILDREN'S PROBLEM is peer pressure when they go to school AND HEAR the smooth talk that OTHER CHILDREN talk, it influences them. so they feel left out, and in order to be

accepted by them, they feel that they have to

follow the crowd and

forget about what their parents taught them.

BUT WHAT I WILL TELL CHILDREN THE BEST ADVICE IS TO

LISTEN AND OBEY THEIR PARENTS AND THEY WILL HAVE A

GOOD REWARD IN LIVE.

BY LISTENING TO THEIR PARENTS THEY WILL NOT DO DRUGS

OR DRINK ALCOHOL

5/10/99

Bonnie Lee Young

When I Was Young, I Dreamed About...

6/29/98

When I was young growing up in Georgia walking among the beautiful trees I always dreamed and looked forward to become educated because when you are educated you can be very helpful to others as well as yourself.

If you apply to yourself the things you learn while you are in school, you will be able to help

others to read and write the same as your

teacher helps you to read and write. I want to be

comprehensive with my dream so one will be

able to understand what I am saying. For an

example, a T.V. talk show host once said a

gentleman told her he liked the way she

talked.

For her being educated and speaking well, he

gave her a job. So we can see from her example

we can do the same. For myself, I want to be a

counselor of law and be able to help children

and fly around the world. Now I dream about a

world where people are living in peace and

loving one another and giving glory to God.

Bonnie Lee Young

So the King tells the Queen

I love the way you dance

Just like dew falls from

Heaven and saturates the

Field, so your dancing does

To me.

Dance Hall

They are all at the dance hall and

They are dancing. So the Queen

Tells the King to lay down his cane

And I will give you a swing in the

Ring. And let them see us swing

The same in the rain. First we will

Do the rumble until there is no

More rum.

10/14/98

<u>Sold</u>

Although the Lokie plantation had been sold, and the house was remodeled, however the surrounding where Mary and I played did not changed. I will never forget the togetherness and happiness that Mary and I had on this plantation seen on the picture. I visited Mary in 1998. We were happy to see each other. It was my first time seeing Mary since 1948. She is doing fine and enjoying her own home. Like me, she is talking and thinking about her father's plantation, but now it is sold.

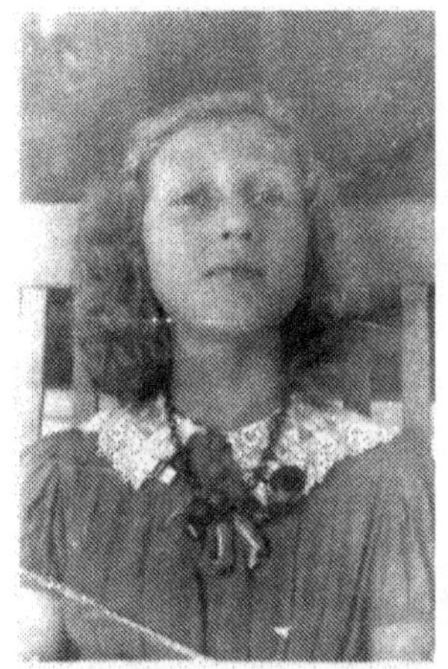

Mary

The plantation

<u>Visit</u>

Grandchildren visit the farm in the summer time and enjoy their play ground, and the surrounding beautiful trees. Rosa: left Ruth and Priscilla: right. Great grandchildren under the trees. They love and appreciate the hard work their grandparents did for them.

Great grandchildren

Moving Forward in Life Despite Adversities: Part II.

(Continuing from Part I, with my sister Vera)

Vera wrote me and told me the bad conditions she was living under in Georgia (although she was there with Willie and my dad). In the letter she asked me to send for her. At the time I was living with my cousin in Harlem. I understood what Vera was going through. I lived under a lot of pressure, while living there in Georgia with my stepmother also. So much so, I ran away from home to my older sister Rubbie's home, (who also lived in Georgia). I told Rubbie the pressure I was living under and she listened to my plea, and looking me in the eyes with eyes of understanding she said to me: "I understand the pain and suffering you're going through." Rubbie was sympathetic to me. Rocking and holding her baby (me) in her arms, she said quietly "I am going to use wisdom and take you back home to your father, because home is the right place for you to be."

So I agreed to go back home with her. While we were there she talked with our father and told him that it was good on his part to listen to his wife. On the other hand, she said, "You should also take into consideration your children when they plead to you." Being an understanding father, he acknowledged that and said that Rubbie was right. He said, "you know, daughter, when you work hard eight hours a day you just don't think right." My sister Rubbie said she understood. So daddy and Rubbie kissed and showed love to each other. For a while, being back home things went well. Then suddenly trouble stirred up again. My stepmother just had to have her domineering ways. For peace's sake when we went to the field to work, I would not come home from work for lunch. I stayed and wept furiously under a shady tree on the side of the row.

I understood the pressure my daddy was under. He just bought his plantation and he had the responsibility of paying our mother's hospital bill and my sister leaving home pregnant, which he found out after it happened. My daddy was a loving father. But going through situations, and knowing his situations, I realized as a young girl my father was under this pressure from a nagging domineering wife. So I really understood Vera's situation. So, when she sent me that letter asking me to send for her, I sent for her. She came to stay with my cousin and me in Harlem.

While we were there in Harlem, my husband was away overseas in the United States Marines, so Vera and I shared a room together. At night Vera would talk and tell me how she was scolded and beaten by our domineering stepmother. I listened to her as she talked to me so I could help her to put her under my wing in a sense and help her until she got a job, and that she did. She got a very good job working at the Post Office, and is still presently there. She is also happily married. Talking to her husband about her, he thanked me for helping her. This is what he said…

<u>In search for a Christian Wife:</u> (Clarence

Woods)

"My search for a Christian wife, one that feared and worshipped Jehovah God, was a wonderful quest and experience. I was blessed in 1966 when starting to attend meetings at a new Kingdom Hall and enjoying the meetings arranged there, I came to know the young woman I would come to love and marry and through that union my life has been satisfying and complete. Let me explain the way it happened. On attending one meeting I was introduced to this very beautiful attractive sister who measured up to all my expectations. And the exciting thing about that was when I first saw her and was being introduced I didn't see any rings on the third finger of her left hand. About two meetings later I asked to see the third finger of her left hand she held out her left hand. I noticed there was no engagement or wedding ring on them. And my heart excitedly began to beat faster. And I said in my heart 'she's the one I'm going to marry.' And so I began the quest to make her my wife, which became a reality in 1977.

Though there was some years waiting for the marriage to come about, it was worth it. The waiting caused our love to grow stronger and stronger. And we, my wife Vera and I have grown in love for Jehovah God and his arrangement for marriage down through the years. In fact, for the past 24 years, Vera and I have continually enjoyed great happiness and Jehovah's blessings.

<u>How did I feel?</u>

Despite all the adversities she faced, I am happy for her, because she never turned to drugs or became a drunkard. She found a good husband and now they are serving Jehovah together.

Mr. And Mrs. Woods

Moved

Daddy made his move from the local plantation to his own plantation. He was walking around the grounds and suddenly he said "I am going to buy my own plantation." So when he told us that he was going to buy his own plantation our hearts jumped for joy and we said "yes Dad we are glad for you," and he said "The reason why I am buying my own plantation is for my boys to have their own place.

When I was growing up in life the "Boss Man" would always come around and tell my Mother to get me out of bed and send me out into the field and get me married my wife I have sons and no one is going to dominate my sons. So we all agreed. Then he said "Children, my problem is that I am engulfed with bills but my brother Sterling is to help support me for awhile. Then he said "I tell you children the land is not producing now but it will over the years after it is cultivated.

<u>Rubbie</u>

As I stated in Part I, Rubbie is my oldest sister. She is a very outstanding woman. She is kind, sensitive, loving, caring. Rubbie followed my mother's example. She was easy to be taught by my mother. She sewed, she knitted, she made quilts, and by her being such a loving and obedient person, when she was given in marriage, my parents gave her the most beautiful wedding you would want to see. Her guests numbered four hundred. She got married at home and what a sight to see! The way my mom decorated the porch—in fine linen. And when she walked out of the room that is what she walked on, fine linen. Her gown was expensive. She had one girl to carry her veil; she had a maid of honor, who was our sister in law, Ozzie. She had bridesmaids and she had flowers galore. Her gifts, you could not number because there were so many. After she got married, she gave birth to eight children. Six girls, two boys. They all finished high school and some of them went to college. They all have good jobs, serving in high capacities.

Some went to Chicago to live. Her sons Alvin Young Cook and Robert Cook went to Hartford,

Connecticut. They both have good government jobs, and they are happily married. Alvin is on the picture above, along with Pricilla his first cousin. They also lived in Fort Gaines, Georgia, and they have their own homes and land. Sad to say, my sister Rubbie died in 1987.

<u>My brother Cleo</u>

My brother Cleo got married to Ozzie (the maid of honor to my sister Rubbie). They brought forth six children: four girls, and two boys. They are all educated, and working and serve in high capacities. Cleo is still there in Fort Gaines, overseeing the land, and he is doing a very good job. He has the land rented out; it is all paid for now, and divided between him and my brother David Young.

**David is discussing how the land
should be divided**

Cleo

<u>My brother David</u>

David was a very fortunate one in life. He
prospered. Everything he put his hand on seemed to
turn into gold. After our mother died, he moved to
Florida to help our father with the farm. He is now
happily married and has his own home. He is still
helpful toward the farm, traveling back and forth from

Florida to Georgia. As seen in the picture above, he is talking about how they're going to divide the land. Before my father died, he made out a deed for the land for Cleo, David, and his son Willie. And happy to say, they welcomed the girls back whenever they decided to return home.

<u>My brother Willie</u>

Willie stayed home longer than any of us, and helped my father with the farm. After my daddy had paid for the land, Willie decided that he would go to Florida. He got married to Agnes, and they brought forth two young men. They now have good jobs and are doing fine. My brother, though, had a bad accident on his job, and he could not work for a while, but he never gave up on reaching his goal. He continued on until he bought his wife the home that he wanted to give her from the start, before his accident. He was well liked by our stepmother though. So, one year, I visited him and his wife, and we were talking about our stepmother, how domineering she was. We couldn't understand why she treated us the way she did.

But years passed, and I visited my brother Willie in Florida and he told me that he learned that she believed in spiritism and witchcraft. So I did not tell the rest of the family what he related to me. But constantly I told them to demolish the house, but they did not. However, eventually they listened to my plea and they burned the house down and it is much more pleasant there now. My brother Willie was a very positive person. That is why I have taken the time out to talk to him about our stepmother. Knowing him from the time we all lived together in Georgia, he was always the center of attention in the family. He kept all of us laughing. Although my mother was beautiful, and my father was handsome when they was young (I thought), but yet and still Willie would just talk about them to their face, and call them ugly, and say he did not know where they came from. He would call them out of their names, not mom and dad. I cannot recall him ever getting a beating from my mom or dad.

<u>Willie and the guys</u>

When we moved to Fort Gaines, Willie and the guys joined together going from house to house laughing, making fun of people, and telling them "Come out of your house, your house is on fire!" And whatever there was to frighten people, they did it. And girls loved him. As funny and joking as he was, he was chicken when it came to girls, because he wasn't ready for marriage. Sad to say, he died in 1997.

Continuing with my domineering

stepmother

Now, after we all left home, our domineering stepmother pursued her domineering ways with our daddy. She wanted him to give her son an acre of land so that he could have a house built on it. My father agreed to do so, but his sons disapproved.

They said it would bring about a conflict. Although my father had signed over the acre of land to her son, and made it legal, my brothers went and had it stopped by law, saying that my father was senile, and didn't know what he was doing. When they did this our stepmother really went into a rage. My father was sick at the time this happened. So she said, since your sons can dominate over you, I will show you what I will do for you." She snatched the pillow from under his head while he was lying there sick, and could not help himself, and she took everything out of the house and left him laying there flat in the bed, sick.

What action was taken?

My oldest sister Rubbie called us and told us to come home to take care of our daddy. It's not that she

didn't want to help, but she had her hands full with her children. So we took turns going home to see about him, and what the family decided to do was have my oldest brother take him into his house. Then later, my sister Rubbie was able to watch over him and take care of him during the day while by brother was at work. Because by now, my brother was not farming any longer, but was working for the State. Our daddy was never forsaken. We helped him until he died in 1974.

<u>My concern</u>

My concern was the trees, because I liked to climb trees and crack eggs in the bird's nests. One day my mother asked me "If you keep cracking those eggs, how do you think more birds are going to come." I took that into consideration. The land is near a beautiful park, boating, nature, wildlife, fishing and camping, and if you liked to dance by the light of the moon, you could. So, again, not that we did not appreciate what our father did, we were very grateful for what he did. He did just what a loving father would do.

<u>What was our problem?</u>

When we moved from the Lokey's plantation to Historical Fort Gaines, Georgia, our house was not as nice as the house we lived in on the Lokey's plantation. The problem was that we were disappointed with the house. When we looked up at the ceiling and saw the stars at night, we would say many times "only if our mother were living, things would be better," because she always went for the best, the best of everything, or nothing. She worked very hard and saw that everything went well with our daddy. Her work was around the clock. If she was not working with our daddy, she was busy making our clothes and teaching us about God.

<u>Daddy prospered</u>

Although we did not like the house that was on the land that our father bought for us to live in, we are all happy now because the move our father made was not in vain. Daddy prospered. Now they have a new house, no more looking up at the ceiling and seeing the stars at night, no more carrying water and cooking on wooden stoves, no more outside toilets or tin-top house. Daddy prospered from the land. Sweet potatoes, corn peanuts, and more. Daddy moving forward was profitable. Daddy had a sound mind and knew what he was doing for his children in the future. He had an A-model, and T-model Ford car to take us around to and fro. We told him to get rid of the car and buy a new one because the children in school were laughing at us.

<u>How were the Young's known?</u>

The Young's were known in Georgetown by that T-model Ford. When daddy would drive us into Georgetown, to Mr. Wood's store, everyone would stand around and say: "Here come the Youngs in that T-model Ford." Mr. Wood was a friend of daddy's. When daddy would drive up in front of his store, Mr. Wood would say "These are Tip Young's children, let them come in and have what they want." So there was no escaping being noticed. Responding to our asking him to get rid of the car he said: "A T-model and A-model ford will take you the same place as a Cadillac, but the difference is that the Cadillac will run faster." "So I take care of my business, and I leave other people's business alone, so likewise that is the way it should be." All in all, we children enjoyed travelling with our daddy in the T-model Ford. The problem was, while the children laughed at us, my father was the only one who had a T-model ford at that time, and the children who laughed at us were not as wealthy as we were. Because like I said before, my daddy prospered. While other people were living on other people's plantations and working, my daddy worked on his own land. He had his ups and downs, but he continued moving forward in life until he obtained what he wanted for his sons—for them to have a place to live. Because the man that I mentioned in Part I, who stood over him and told his mother to send him to the field, was his daddy. But his father didn't prepare a place for him or his brothers. Considering what our father had accomplished, we got over the laughs and got on with our lives.

William giving affection to his own

<u>My son, William</u>

My son, William, was born October 31, 1955 in Flower 5th Avenue Hospital. On the 29th I went into labor. Early that Friday morning, my cousin took me to the hospital, the doctor examined me, and said I was having false labor pains. They sent me back home, and told me to keep count of the time between the pains. So I did. That Friday night the pains came just as they said they would. So my husband got a cab and we went back to the hospital. The doctor's examined me a second time, and said the same thing that they were false labor pains. I went back home and the pains got so severe that my husband and I called a cab again and we went back to the hospital. This time the doctor stayed there in the examining room with me. This time he said "oh no, I am keeping you this time, I'm not sending you back." So they called the nurse told her to make arrangements to take me upstairs. So they took me upstairs. They assigned one doctor and one nurse to be with me throughout my labor. So throughout that Saturday night I was in hard Labor. So now, it's

Sunday morning October 31st, I started having pains in my chest, so I yelled out that I was having pains in my chest, and the nurse ran and called the doctors and they came in. I did not know how many doctors were around my bed.

While they were there treating my heart attack, my water broke, and they gave me medication, and behind that I got so sleepy and relaxed. They started tapping me on my face telling me "stay awake, stay awake." The next thing I knew, they were pushing me into the labor room. They realized that I could not have a natural birth, so they took my baby by force, because I was too sick to have a Caesarian section. The next thing I knew the nurse came and told me that she had a guest for me. That guest was my husband, coming in with a beautiful bunch of flowers, but he didn't stay long because he realized that I was sick and weak. He showed me affection and thanked me for bringing such a beautiful son into the world. The nurse came into the room after he left, and asked me if I wanted to see my baby. I did not know if I wanted to see my baby or not, because I had so many bad labor pains. So I said slowly "Yeeeessss."

So, when she brought the baby to me, my heart leaped for joy, and I thanked God for my healthy baby. Then I stayed in the hospital for seven days, and then my husband and I came home so happy with our healthy baby. We enjoyed watching him grow up and now it was time for him to go to school. He was a brilliant student. His goal was to be a professional basketball player. He broke his leg twice and the doctor said he would not be able to play professional basketball. All in all, when he turned nineteen and went to West Palm Beach, Florida, he got a job working with computers, and from there he worked at Channel Eleven in the newsroom, then after that he decided he would come back home, in 1984. In 1997, he fell asleep in death.

<u>Tobe Young Other Children</u>

The Young family was a very large family, because my grandfather Tobe Young had children other than by his wife Isabelle. One of his sons was named David Young. David Young's wife gave birth to Cleveland Young and this is what Cleveland stated to me about his family life:

"I was born February 22, 1921 in Clayton Alabama, in Barrour County. My mother and father raised eight children. Two girls and six boys all of my family attended religious services regularly. Mother and father taught us to live by the golden rule. 'Do unto others as you would have them do unto you.' In the early 1930's my family bought a billy goat, male goat, colored black and white. We named him Spot. He did not like small children. One day, I was going to the mailbox, and the billy goat was grazing grass. He looked up at me, and then put his head down and charged me. I took off running as fast as I could. Mother was standing on the front porch. Mother yelled: "run, son!" He almost caught me before I reached the porch. Mother grabbed me stared at me, put her arms around me and went into the house. We went into the house; the billy goat went away where he was at the rest of the time eating grass. Mother and father talked it over about Spot the goat. They decided, before he hurt someone in the family, that they would kill him. In those days there were no refrigerators, but we did own an icebox. It held 150 pounds of ice along with the billy goat. That way we kept food from spoiling.

All of my family was hard working people. We all were gifted. My father worked in a coal mine in

Birmingham, Alabama. He told the family about the coals above the head would fall down, but they built a scaffold to support the falling coal. Father would visit the family two weeks in the month. In 1930 we moved out of the city to the country 7 miles away. Still Clayton was our city. Barbour county. The family started farming, we raised lots of different things. We raised chickens, 150-200 chickens. My father built chicken houses for them to sleep in at night. Inside the chicken house he also built a ramp for the chickens. At night sometime the chickens would wander around in the woods getting lost, never finding their way home. Hawks would fly down from the sky and catch the chickens, and fly way with them. We also raised turkeys. Of course they have to be fed and watered, and they like to eat. We raised pigs also.

That was in the middle of 1920. And sometime during those years we would kill 4 or 5 hogs in a year's time. Father built smokehouses to keep the meat he made. Smoked meat, sugar-cured meat, and mother made stuffed sausages and plain sausages. Also, such meats as we see in the grocery store today, mother made. She also made crackling from the hog's skin, and pickled hogs feet too. We lost lots of hogs in those days, when crops were being gathered. In those days people turned their hogs lose. There was a man and his son that would get together and steal lots of our hogs. Father watched this man and his sons round up the hogs, and catch hogs. They tied their feet together and strapped them to a pole and would take the hog away. The next day father went by the man's house. The man invited father in his house. After inviting father he asked father to have dinner with the family. His wife had cooked dinner. He told father we have fresh meat, hog meat for dinner. Sitting down at the dinner table the man told father how good the meat was. Did he like the meat? Father told the man the meat you are eating is mine. The man was surprised that my father own the hogs that he stole. We raised corn of different types: Sweet corn, white corn, and yellow corn. My father built cribs to keep and store the corn away. We used to shuck the corn shell off of the corn and make corn meal and grits.

We raised cotton, and we sold them by the tons. Of course, cotton has to be processed and taken to the cotton mill to have the seeds removed. We also raised peanuts. The cows needed to be fed. I milked cows many days too. By hand we churned the milk, and by hand it took about 45 minutes or 60 minutes for the butter to come to the top. Mother had a molder, it was round. It made cakes of butter. We used a molder, keeping the butter in an ice box, because there was no refrigerator. In the house we lived in there were two big bedrooms, a dining room and kitchen. The house had a fireplace that was heated by wood logs. We used wood burning heaters, a wood burning stove for cooking food. There was no running water, no bathtub. We took baths in a tin tub. Father built a toilet outside 60 feet from the house. Once, when the well went dry, father, being a smart man, used sticks to somehow find the running water. We raised sugar cane, and white cane, but sugar cane was the best and it still is. My father used to take cane to the mill and turned it into juice. There was a big vat we put the juice into, and built a large fire so that the juice would cook until it turned into syrup.

This took hard work and long hours. On the farm we raised cabbage, and turnip greens too. The whole family would work in the field from sun up until sun down. In those days mother and father took the vegetables to town to sell them. We had much to sell in those days. My mother and father taught all of the family to live by the golden rule, and that helped us to be successful. Three of my brothers worked at a sawmill. My older brother operated the sawmill. My brother was the best man for running a sawmill. My other brothers and I stacked the lumber after it was cut. Sometimes we would cut the trees with a crossword saw that took two men to operate correctly. In those days mules were used to pull those logs to a flat bed truck. Then they were mounted on the truck and taken to the sawmill. The logs were cut into timber, which was stored in houses my brother had built just for that purpose. My older brother built them and his granddaughter and her husband still live in one of those houses.

In the late 1930's and 40's I helped build garages that are still standing to this day, located at Fort Benny Georgia. I was the first one in my family to own an automobile. Mother and father talked to the family to work and save some of the money. The first house I bought was in Columbus, Georgia. I bought three in Wisconsin, eight in Detroit Michigan and two in Florida. My wife and I were married August 6th 1947. She died on the 24th of March 1965. My wife and I together had eight children, two girls and 6 boys. I never married again. All of the children eventually went off to college. I raised them myself. I bought two houses, duplexes for my children. My brothers were in the military. Two of them served in World War II.

Three went into the army and one in the Navy. My brother Norman lost his life during World War II. All of my brothers are now deceased with the exception of the youngest, Samuel. I thank my mother and father for helping us to move forward in life despite adversities, and for helping us to see that serving God should be first in our lives.

How did the grandchildren feel about the farm?

The younger generation of the Young family (grandchildren) did not like working on the farm. In 1965, after they finished high school, they left and moved to the big cities that they read about while they were growing up. So there were adversities, but they took them with pleasure. Ann lived with her grandmother. Her name is Addie, until she was twelve years old. Then Ann left and move to Miami, Florida to live with her mother. She attended school there in 1954, and graduated from high school. Then she met her husband Ralph, and they got married. Ann and her husband Ralph brought forth four children, three girls, and one boy. They raised all of them in Miami, Florida. Ann is a good mother and a good wife. She had some hard times in her marriage, yet she weathered the storm. She worked hard and educated her children. They all went to school and college. Now they are working, and enjoying life in Miami, Florida.

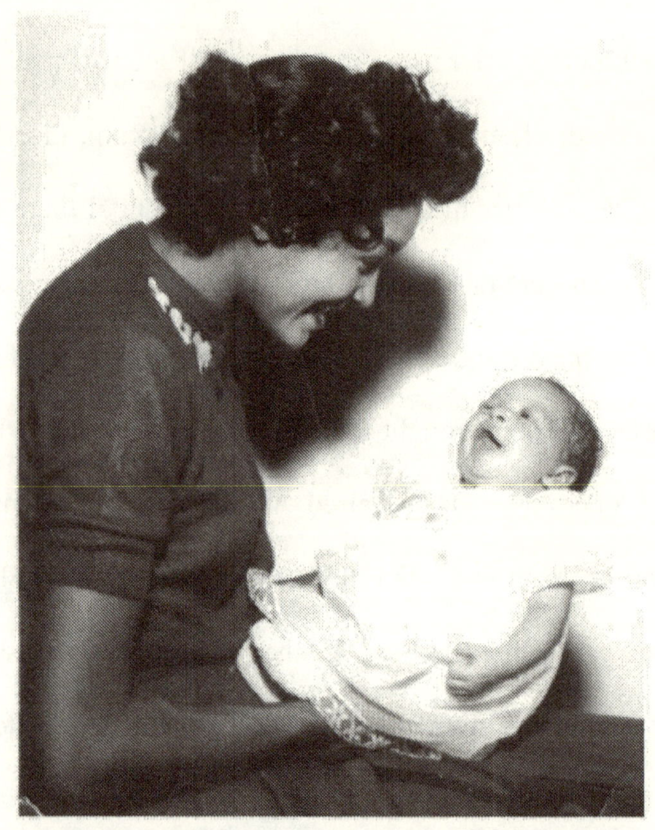

<u>What was Ann's first job?</u>

First, Ann worked as a maid at the Olympia

Theatre for thirteen years, part-time for eighteen

dollars a week. When her baby girl turned four years old, she got a job with the Dade County school board in 1965. She drove a school bus for nineteen years, and in 1984 radios were put on the buses, and she got a dispatcher position. And in 1989 she was promoted to a supervisor position. She supervised over 40 drivers and 24 aides before retiring in August of 1992. She had 26 and a half years of employment with the school board of Dade County. In 1994, she relocated to Fort Gaines, Georgia, and settled down on 60 acres of land that her grandmother left for the family before she died.

Ann, her husband, and her nephew live on the 60 acres now, and they are really enjoying the country air there. When I visit my home, Ann is the one that tours me around to see the beautiful countryside. Neither Fort Gaines, nor Georgetown, Georgia has tall buildings, nor red and green lights, but these two towns are very interesting. Their parks are beautiful. They have boating, natural wildlife, fishing, and camping, and golfing. Fishing is a major attraction for those who come to the lake. People come from a distance to hunt and fish. There are lots of summer homes on the Patula Creek Lake. You would enjoy their beautiful sunny side. When I was living there, I liked these two small towns. We country girls would write and tell each other when we were going to town. We did not have a telephone to call one another, so we would write and tell all of our friends to meet us in the big city.

<u>Eufaula</u>

Eufaula, Alabama was our big city. We would meet in this city on Saturday's. We would be so glad to see each other. We would greet each other, walk around in the street and buy hamburgers. We were not being disrespectful when we would walk in the street and eat the hamburgers. Back in the 50's colored people were not allowed to sit down and eat in a restaurant. That's right, back in the 1950's we were called "colored folks". We didn't mind it, we were so glad to see each other. What a difference it is now when you go there. You can eat anywhere you chose. And what a blessing this is from God. One thing I like about the people in Fort Gaines and Georgetown is that they are very friendly. When you visit there, they welcome you with kindness, and when you are leaving they'll say: "Please come back again."

<u>Visit to my hometown in 1998</u>

When I visited my hometown in Georgia in 1998, I asked my older brother Cleo to take me to the Lokey Plantation. I knew that the plantation was sold. When we drove up in the yard, to my surprise, the house was remodeled. Much the same, but remodeled. Very beautiful as you can see from the picture above. The young man that bought the plantation was very nice and kind when we drove up in the yard. He came out and asked "May I help you folks?" We said "Yes, we once lived here, and we want to look around and see the plantation." He said, "yes, by all means help yourself." So, we did.

We got out of the truck and walked around, and took some pictures of the house and the land. Seeing the beauty of the land, pretty trees, birds singing beautiful songs, you get that same feeling you had when you were living there. Only thing was missing was the fourteen houses that the people lived in were all demolished. The only people that lived there were the young man that welcomed us, his wife and his son. As we were looking around, I didn't see the windmill, so I asked him what had happened to it. But he said he couldn't keep it because a storm blew it away. So we sat there and we talked to him about how things were when we lived there, how much we enjoyed the land and how nice the Lokey family was.

But, when we were getting ready to leave, he said "Wait a minute, let me call my wife." So, he called his wife and said "come out hon, I want you to meet some folks that once lived here." So, she did. She came out and she too was a very nice lady, very hospitable. She had taken time out and explained to us how they bought the land. We talked for a while. So I said to her "Let me take your picture to put in my book that I'm writing." She said, "Oh, no, I look too bad." I told her, "That is what makes the picture interesting." She said, "Oh no, I still don't want you to take my picture. You can take my son's picture if you like." So she put him on the ground so I could take his picture. We all laughed. Now we thought it was time for us to go, we did not want to wear out our welcome. So we told them we were leaving. They too asked us to come back again. I told them that I lived in New York, but my brother Cleo still lived in Georgia. He said. "That's where you live? I visited there once, I don't think I'll be coming back any time soon." So we left, my brother and I. But before we left, I stepped aside and said a silent prayer to Jehovah, thanking Him that I got to know Him. When I lived there at the

Lokey plantation I did not know Him. But through a Bible study, after I left the plantation, I got to know Him.

That was one of the reasons why I wanted to put my feet on that soil, because I walked around lots of days wondering about him, wondering why we had to die, and leave that beautiful greenery there. Now although my grandmother told us God's proper name as I stated in chapter one, I couldn't remember because I was young. When my sister Daisy told Vera, my youngest sister, and me, that we were going to die, we starting crying and crying and crying. She told us while we were living there at the Lokey plantation that we were going to die and decay and I couldn't understand why God would put us in such a beautiful place and take us away. After Daisy told us this, I began on my search for God. I learned from the

Genesis account that it wasn't God's purpose for us to die, but that we should live so long as we obeyed him. And that is what He told Adam. Now I know that he made a sacrifice for us, and that we are going to live in his own due time, because that is what he purposed. So after I had prayed, I was ready to leave.

How did I feel?

Leaving the plantation, going to the road, looking to the left, the two-room schoolhouse that I attended was gone. I got a sad feeling as we were driving away, that we were not living there anymore, remembering the happy days we did have there when we did live there. So now, my brother and I toured around visiting other plantations and people's courtesy and hospitality was outstanding throughout the visit. What an exciting visit!

<u>Vein Occlusion</u>

In chapter one, I stated why I left my professional trade (barbering), because I had a vein occlusion in my eyes. I always had a problem with my eyes, from an early age. I had my eyes examined every year by a professional optomologist. One morning, when I woke up and looked in the mirror my eyes were red. Right away I said to myself, let me call my doctor. During the time I was getting dressed to go to the doctor, to my surprise, when I looked in the mirror again, they had cleared up. So, then I became my own doctor, and said to myself that my eyes were just tired from hard work. So I went on to work taking care of my customers and enjoying my work to the full. Six months passed and my eyes turned red again. This time I called Manhattan Eye and Ear Hospital, and they told me to come in and have my eyes examined.

<u>So I did</u>

After the doctors examined my eyes, they told me my eyes had been bleeding and from the bleeding, a blood clot was left behind my eyes. The doctor said not to worry about it. He said 'the body will take care of itself, and the blood clot would go away from behind your eyes.' Several months passed, and I started seeing lights in front of my eyes. Again I called the doctor and they told me to come in right away. This time the doctor's ordered that pictures be taken of my eyes. After the pictures were taken he read the report and told me that I had to have laser surgery. If not, I would lose one of my eyes. So they did not let me go home from the hospital that day. They started the laser surgery and they told me to take it easy for a while, that meant no work. The surgery turned out well, but I was not able to cut hair anymore, because I wanted to be honest with my customers.

<u>I decided</u>

What I decided to do then was to look for jobs in another field. I joined the union, and in less than a week they called me for a job working in the hospital. I realized that my eyes were not in a good condition to take the job. Since my eyes were not up to par for working, I applied for my retirement Social Security. After I started receiving my Social Security checks I realized that I was a person that worked all of my life, and couldn't just sit home and look forward to a Social Security check. I prayed to Jehovah and asked him to use me in his way. So I went to the Kingdom Hall and asked the elders to give me a form for Regular Pioneer Service, (which is a form of full-time service requiring 90 hours a month, that one has a good standing with Jehovah). After I filled out the form, and turned it in to the congregation, within a month I was approved to serve as a regular pioneer.

I was very happy and thankful to Jehovah that he had answered my prayer and approved for me to be a

Regular Pioneer in his service. I was already serving Jehovah since 1959, when I was baptized, but In March 1990, I started Regular Pioneering going from door to door and on the streets, for 90 hours each month. And all of our work for Jehovah is voluntary, not for profit. In 1991, I was privileged to go to Pioneer Service School for two weeks, to better equip myself with the scriptures. I can truly say that there is no greater happiness than talking to people about Jehovah's purpose for man. Just like I enjoyed going to bed at night thinking about going to take care of my customers, I feel even more so about my service for Jehovah.

In conclusion, I can truly say that the Young family is thankful to our Grandma Isabella for helping us to move forward in life despite adversities we faced, and as for me, I can truly say just as Habakkuk the prophet said at Habakkuk 3:17-19: "Although the fig tree itself may not blossom, and there may be no yield on the vines; the work of the olive tree may actually turn out a failure, and the terraces themselves may actually produce no food, the flock may actually be severed from the pen, and there may be no herd in the enclosures, yet as for me, I will exult in Jehovah himself, I will be joyful in the God of my salvation."

-Bonnie Lee Young

<u>Kolomoki Mounds</u>

Bonnie is overlooking the top of the Kolomoki Mounds at the State Historic Park. In Georgia. ON top of this mound is where the Indians worshipped. When you visit here you get that relative feeling. I am happy that I visited the Kolomoki Mounds to see some of the evidence that our grandmother taught us about.

Bobbie

<u>Ceiling</u>

My nephew Bobbie appreciates his grandfather for moving forward in life despite the adversities he faced. "I was not born when my grandfather bought his land, but I am not perplexed. My Grandfather taught and educated me about the land, the condition of the house when he bought it, and how my father, Cleo, and he worked to cultivate the land. "Farming," Bobbies said, "is security in life, now and in the future. We do not have a mansion but we have a home. No more looking up at the ceiling and seeing the stars at night."

Bobbie liked to visit the Indian Kolomoki mounds, to read and learn about his great grandmother's ancestors. Bobbie also like to go fishing.

ABOUT THE AUTHOR

Bonnie Young currently lives in Brooklyn, New York. She enjoys writing poetry and studying the bible, furthering her education and teaching others about God's incoming government.

My grandmother was an electrifying lady so much she inspired me to write this book about her and other.